IMAGES OF ENGLAND

DONCASTER
REVISITED

IMAGES OF ENGLAND

DONCASTER
REVISITED

PETER TUFFREY

TEMPUS

*This book is dedicated to
all the photographers who
have made this book possible.*

Frontispiece: Congregational Church, Hall Gate, situated between Prince's Street and Bradford Row. Built in 1804, the structure underwent considerable alterations in around 1896. Local architect J.G. Walker was responsible for the work which enabled the building to seat 900 people.

First published 2004

Tempus Publishing Limited
The Mill, Brimscombe Port,
Stroud, Gloucestershire, GL5 2QG
www.tempus-publishing.com

© Peter Tuffrey, 2004

The right of Peter Tuffrey to be identified as the Author
of this work has been asserted in accordance with the
Copyrights, Designs and Patents Act 1988.

All rights reserved. No part of this book may be reprinted
or reproduced or utilised in any form or by any electronic,
mechanical or other means, now known or hereafter invented,
including photocopying and recording, or in any information
storage or retrieval system, without the permission in writing
from the Publishers.

British Library Cataloguing in Publication Data.
A catalogue record for this book is available from the British Library.

ISBN 0 7524 3233 8

Typesetting and origination by Tempus Publishing Limited.
Printed and bound in Great Britain.

Contents

	Introduction	7
	Acknowledgements	8
one	Around the Town	9
two	Shops	33
three	Pubs and Clubs	49
four	Buildings	57
five	Transport	61
six	Events	71
seven	Formal Groups	91
eight	Redevelopment	103
nine	Aerials	117

The demolition of the Young Man's Christian Association building at the Cleveland Street/St Sepulchre Gate junction c. 1963. The YMCA was originally constructed as a hospital in 1853 by George Dunn. It provided facilities for people in Doncaster for many years until it became the YMCA headquarters.

Introduction

It is almost ten years since I compiled the first *Central Doncaster* in 1995, my first book for the publishers, and I was very pleased that it sold well. I felt that it contained pictures not seen before and quite informative captions and that these aspects went some way towards its success. I was also flattered last year when the publishers decided to revamp and reprint it along with a number of their other successful early titles.

So I suppose in some ways the stage was set to produce a second volume, which was thankfully encouraged by Tempus. In compiling the work I have kept to some of the picture categories used in the first volume and have endeavoured to choose photographs that have not been reproduced hitherto in similar publications.

The pictures date from around 1870 to the mid-1990s and I have chosen such an expanse of time, in photographic terms, because I feel that Doncaster is a town where constant change is a regular feature – though whether this has always been for the good has been a constant matter of debate, it has been interesting nevertheless. When I produced the first *Central Doncaster* there was great outrage when the old Infirmary in Whitaker Street was demolished as part of the development which saw the colossal DHSS building erected – this too at a time when the 'Donnygate' scandal was smothering the town.

At the present time of writing, the town is undergoing further upheaval with the construction of a new passenger interchange. The work being undertaken for this has seen a number of relatively new buildings (some seen in the course of construction in this and the first book) demolished in the name of progress. Also in the years separating these publications we have seen another massive development in the construction of a 'new' North Bridge. But perhaps Doncaster's central position in the country, in easy reach of all points of the compass, makes it not surprising that constant change has to take place for whatever reasons.

I am pleased to include pictures that I have recently discovered; the main 'little gem', it has to be said, is the picture of the Arcadia, now the Local Authority's

Civic Theatre. Whilst I have quite a collection of pictures featuring Doncaster and Doncaster District cinemas, the one of the Arcadia has constantly eluded me. Perhaps inevitably it is from the lens of Edgar Leonard Scrivens, a giant amongst the district's postcard photographers. Another picture, the interior of the NatWest Bank on High Street, is also a curious rarity. I say this because it is extremely rare to see interior views of banks, given the high security risk posed. It is also interesting to compare the interior layout from when the picture was taken, probably in the mid-1920s when the bank was first opened, to how it is today. Some of my favourite pictures include the aerial views because they reveal so much about areas as they were and show how they have changed.

Whilst Doncaster remains a town of change, it is inevitable that books of this type will remain a source of great interest to people of all ages. And it is up to each one of us to look and see if the changes, which have been brought upon us by successive generations, are for the better or for the worse.

Acknowledgements

I would like to thank the following people for their help: Eric Braim, Ken Elliff, Hugh Parkin.

one

Around the Town

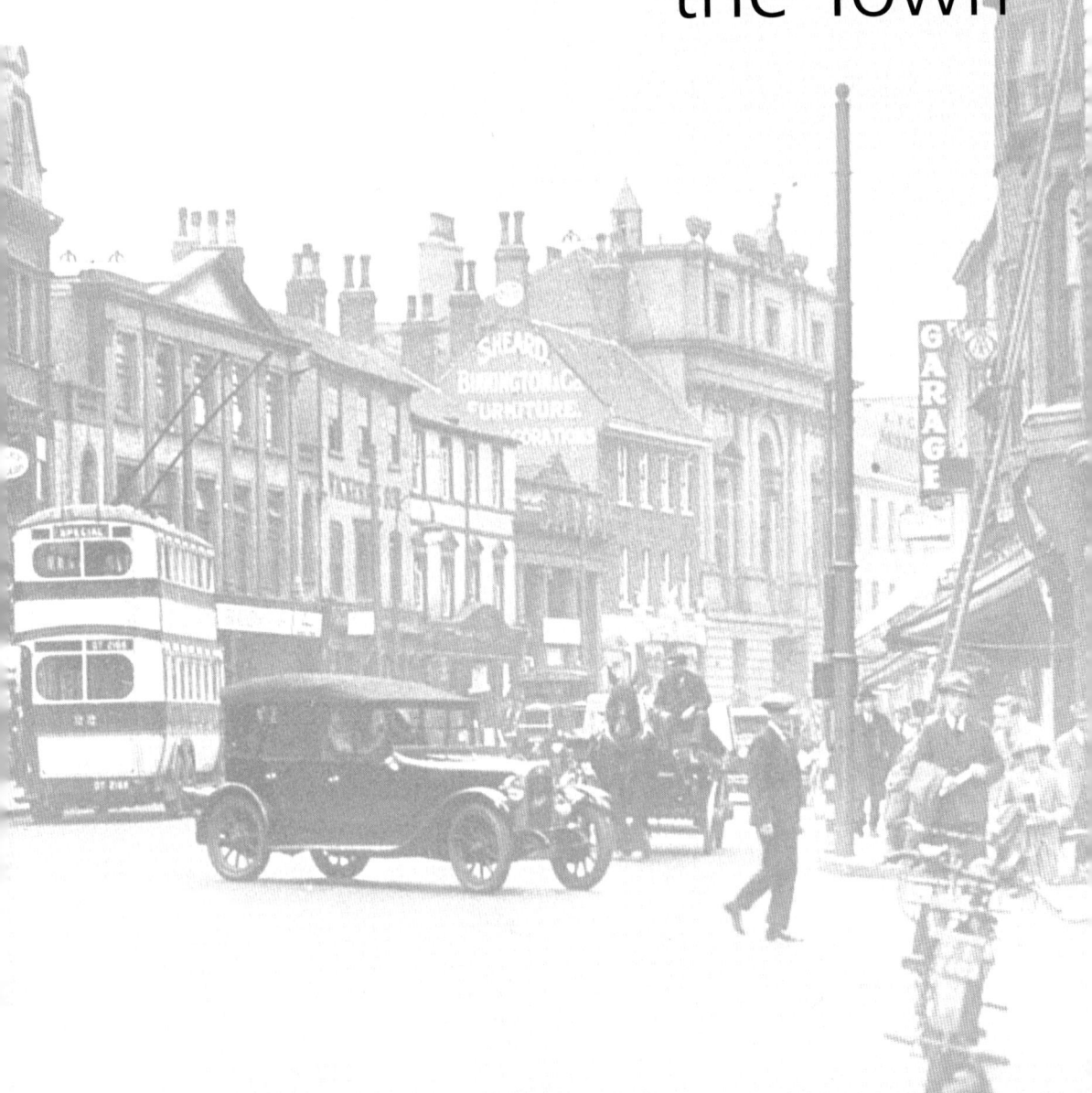

A group of properties at the St James Street/St Sepulchre Gate junction. They include the business premises of Foulstones and the Alma Inn public house. The latter premises, which dated from at least 1860, were rebuilt in 1936 and demolished during 1966.

Bawtry Road on a section of the Great North Road looking north.

Bennetthorpe, which also formed a part of the Great North Road, looking south with new house construction on the left. Bennethorpe takes its name from Jospeh Bennett who once occupied property in the area during the late eighteenth century.

Carr House Road looking east with the Park Hotel on the right. Note that the picture was taken before houses were built on the left. The Park Hotel dates from the mid-1920s when it took the licence of the Wood Street Hotel, which was demolished to facilitate street widening in the town centre.

The Cattle Market with Copley Road and Nether Hall in the distance.

Chequer Road looking towards Carr House Road with a church in the distance. To the right is the Municipal High School for Girls, which was built in around 1910 on part of a site formerly occupied by Chequer House. The High School was enlarged in 1922.

Right: Another view of the Coal Wharf and Hanley's Mill during the 1970s. Mike Taylor, in his book *Memories of the Sheffield and South Yorkshire Navigation* (1988), states: 'The Sheffield and South Yorkshire Navigation was modernised in the early 1980s in anticipation of growing commercial use which has yet to materialise. Indeed trade on the S&SYN has continued to diminish well into the 1990s and there are no "regular" traffics on any part of the forty-three miles of the navigation between Keadby, on the Trent, and Sheffield itself'. The area seen here has since been redeveloped.

Below: 'Tom Puddings' at the Coal Wharf, near Dockin Hill with Hanley's Mill in the background. Hanley's endured two fires during their tenure of the mill – one in 1881 and a second in 1923.

Cleveland Street with the entrance to Baker Street off centre to the left. Traders/business premises featured include the Busy Bee, Bernard Cuttriss's model shop and Harry Clarke's drapery. All the properties were cleared during the early 1960s to make way for the Golden Acres (later Waterdale) Shopping Centre. Busy Bee's premises were formerly occupied by Jim Webb's Stamp Corner and, curiously his sign is still on the building.

The Common or Horseshoe Pond near the Racecourse at the junction of Bennetthorpe and Carr House Road. The view is looking along the stretch which was to become a new section of Carr House Road. The picture was taken in around 1924, shortly before the pond was dismantled.

The Common Pond near the Racecourse looking towards Bawtry. A motorbus approaching Doncaster Rovers' Belle Vue ground may be seen in the centre. Note the tram track in the foreground. Trams started operating on the Racecourse route on 30 June 1902 and ceased on 20 March 1930, being replaced by trolleybuses.

A busy scene at the High Street/Hall Gate junction with Cleveland Street to the left and Silver Street to the right. Trolleybus No. 22, outside the Danum Hotel, was in service between February 1930 and 31 October 1943. Along with No. 23, it was stored at the Leicester Avenue Depot until December 1944 as a possible replacement for war-damaged vehicles.

Above: Factory Lane with the Co-op in the distance. The Beehive public house, which dates from the 1860s was rebuilt in 1939, and is just visible on the left. The trolleybus is working on the Bentley route. On leaving the Greyfriars Road depot and before commencing services near the Brown Cow public house on the North Bridge, it was customary for the Bentley trolleybuses to travel to their starting point via French Gate, St Sepulchre Gate, Station Road, Factory Lane and Trafford Street.

Left: French Gate looking towards the level crossing in Marshgate. The picture pre-dates the opening of the North Bridge in 1910. The White Hart public house second from the left may be seen undergoing alterations, *c.* 1902.

The North Bridge at the time of completion around 1910. Visible on the left of the picture and outside the newly-built Brown Cow public house is possibly the Doncaster Corporation Tramway's Department's horse-drawn overhead tower wagon. The premises on the right include those of Jackson's garage, the Black Boy public house and R. Elvidge, the butcher's shop.

French Gate and the Guild Hall, with the Green Dragon public house on the left and A. Porter's glass and china premises on the right. The Guild Hall was completed in 1848 and had an imposing Classic-style façade. At one time the building housed the Law Courts and the Police Headquarters. The Green Dragon existed here from around 1833 and closed on Thursday 19 January 1961.

Hall Gate looking south with the Reindeer Hotel on the right and the Prudential Assurance Company Ltd's premises on the left. The Reindeer's existence can be traced back to around 1782. It was altered in around 1837 and was demolished during the early part of 1962. The Prudential building was erected following the demolition of old property at the Silver Street/Hall Gate junction in 1912. The design was carried out by Paul Waterhouse, a president of the Royal Institute of British Architects.

Another view of Hall Gate, featuring the dwellings on the left which were demolished for the construction of the Prudential Assurance building. Note the effigy of a bear suspended from the White Bear public house a little further along from the old property. At this time part of the latter was tenanted by the tobacconist, Daniel Portergill.

On the right, D. Portergill's premises, at the Silver Street/Hall Gate junction, are seen from another angle, facing north. The shop, belonging to Martin & Son, may be seen on the opposite side of the junction (at the High Street/Silver Street corner). Note in the foreground the double tracks of the Racecourse tram route which was single tracked from the town centre terminus in Station Road town to the Mansion House in High Street. From there however, the remainder of the route was double tracked.

High Fisher Gate with Lower Fishergate running to the right. The façade of the Ye Olde Crown is just visible on the left while Hanley's Mill dominates much of the picture. While reporting on a huge fire at the mill, the Doncaster Chronicle of 28 September 1923 also divulged the following information: 'The Fishergate Flour Mill was amongst the most important in the Doncaster manufacturing area... the owners in the early days were Messrs Robinson and Hanley, and they were amongst the first in the country to adopt the roller system, this being when the present mill had been erected to replace the old one which was burnt down in 1881. In 1893 Mr Robinson's interest in the firm was bought out by the late Mr Thomas Hanley, whose sons now conduct the business.'

A rare picture of the High Street/Hall Gate junction with the Ram Hotel to the right, c. 1905. Mark Dowson, whose business premises may be seen just behind the Ram, was Mayor in 1897-98. He started his first business as a tailor and outfitter in Catherine Street. He died in 1909. His obituary in the Doncaster Chronicle of 20 August 1909 states: 'His little business in Catherine Street grew rapidly and he soon re-moved to [Hall Gate], where his personal force of character and pushing enterprise served him to good purpose, until ultimately 'Mark Dowson' was writ large in golden letters over the new and imposing corner in [Hall Gate] and Cleveland Street...'

Highfield Road is not fully developed and looks towards St Mary's Road. In the Doncaster Civic Trust Newsletter of November 1990, Eric Braim has the following to say about the area's early development: 'In February 1876 the Highfield Estate was advertised as being set out in lots suitable for the erection of villa and other residences. Highfield Road was laid out on the line of an old field path and King's Road and Queen's Road were laid out at right angles to it.' And he also states: 'Highfield Road was extended from its junction with Queen's Road to provide access to Baxter Avenue and the houses opposite the church, with two storeyed Bays [seen on the right], were built by C. Sprakes & Son in 1908.'

The Great Northern Railway Company's level crossing in Marsh Gate facing south and looking along French Gate. St George's Church may be seen on the left. The level crossing was swept away following the construction of North Bridge. Until this time the Bentley trams terminated a short distance away from the crossing on its northern side. On the opposite site, for a short time, a feeder service was operated from Clock Corner to the level crossing. Once the bridge was constructed, trams were able to carry passengers on an uninterrupted journey into the town centre.

Market Place facing north with St George's Church in the distance. On the left is the Bijou cinema, which operated from Christmas Eve 1909 to around December 1922. Much of the area to the right was taken when a market was established.

Market Place. The building on the right later became the Magdalen Hotel in around 1885.

Above: Old properties in Marshgate

Opposite below: A scene on North Bridge shortly before the preliminary opening in 1910. A more formal opening took place during the following year. John Butler & Co. was the main contractor for the bridge's iron sections and produced them at the company's Stanningley Iron Works. The bridge's total cost was around £100,000.

Above: North Bridge roundabout with Jackson's garage nestling in the shadow of St George's Church. E.W. Jackson & Son was founded in 1904 by Edward Walker Jackson, a retired cloth manufacturer from Morley, and his son, Captain Edward Almond Jackson. Jackson's garage earned renown for the hand-built Cheswold car which it first produced in Doncaster just before the First World War. It was named after the culverted little tributary of the river Don. In February 1983 it was announced that an old established Doncaster motor firm was to close, resulting in the loss of twenty jobs. Motor distributors E.W. Jackson & Son was to shut down because the seventy-nine-year-old company had lost its British Leyland Austin Rover franchise.

The Picture House in High Street, featuring a publicity campaign aimed at attracting audiences to its presentation of *Almost a Honeymoon*. The cinema officially opened on 28 September 1914, showing *The Sign of the Cross*. Talkies came to the cinema on 5 August 1929. It closed on 28 October 1967.

Cleveland Street facing west at the junction with Portland Place. Note the Assemblies of God Pentecostal Church just visible on the right. Also to be seen are H. Brown's radio and TV premises (Nos. 102-4 Cleveland Street), the Cleveland General Transport Café, (occupied by Mrs F. Base) and D. Tolan's Sweets and Tobacco shop.

Queen's Road looking north towards Beckett Road at the junction with Highfield Road. The celebrated Doncaster photogrpaher, Edgar Leonard Scrivens, once had his business premises in the stretch of properties on the right at No. 60 Queen's Road.

The crossroads of High Street, Hall Gate, Silver Street and Cleveland Street. Mark Dowson's stores may be seen on the right, while in the distance there is a splendid view along the south side of Silver Street, before the erection of the Palace Theatre (later Essoldo Cinema) in 1911.

The same view as the previous page a few years later with the Palace Theatre clearly visible in the distance. The theatre was converted to a cinema in 1932 and survived until 1962 when the site was redeveloped.

Market Place and soldiers seemingly taking a wash, c. 1916. The scene is set against an interesting backdrop – the buildings include the Little Red Lion public house (centre) and the Black Bull Hotel. The Little Red Lion was rebuilt in 1928, taking on the new title of Olde Castle Hotel.

South Parade facing Hall Gate, with Thorne Road to the right and Waterdale to the left. The Gaumont Cinema which dates from 1934, dominates the picture. The Gaumont replaced the South Parade Cinema, which opened in December 1920 and was renamed the Majestic in 1922. The Gaumont's grand opening ceremony, on 3 September 1934, was performed by the Mayor, Cllr G.H. Ranyard. The film shown on the occasion was *Evergreen*, starring Jessie Mathews. The Gaumont was re-styled as the Odeon on 20 January 1987.

Bennetthorpe looking towards Elmfield Park. Note in the foreground the tracks of the Racecourse tram route.

St James Street looking towards the town centre. The roads to the right include Oxford Street and Bond Street.

St Sepulchre Gate with Clock Corner in the distance. Dennis Roberts, whose business premises may be seen on the right, was born in 1811. He was the son of a farmer and grazier, at Ragnall near Retford. When he was fourteen, his father sent him to be an apprentice for the Doncaster linen and woollen draper, Matthew Wilton. On completing the apprenticeship, Dennis established a drapery business in Everton, near Bawtry. He combined that with selling groceries and tea. In about 1840 he returned to Doncaster, taking over a Market Place shop. Dennis's son Walter joined his father in business in 1873. Later they moved to 21 St Sepulchre Gate and founded the firm of Dennis Roberts & Son. The business grew, and in 1890 three adjoining shops were purchased and a new building scheme was undertaken.

Station Road facing the Grand Theatre. The road was only twenty years old when it was utilised as a tram terminus in 1902. From St Sepulchre Gate it formed a new approach to the railway station and contained many impressive buildings. A tram bound for the Hexthorpe outer terminus in Bramworth Road may be seen off centre to the right.

Clock Corner, with a view along French Gate c. 1900. The Angel & Royal Hotel is off centre to the left. It is not known who the girls in the picture are, but it is surmised they were going to Sunday School. Clock Corner dates from 1895, when older premises were replaced as part of the widening of Baxter Gate. The new clock tower and premises were constructed to the designs of the architect, J.G. Walker. Robert Farr, whose business was below the clock tower, died in 1908. His obituary in the *Doncaster Gazette* of 27 November 1911, states:
'Deceased was born in Baxter Gate in 1833, where his father carried on the business of an ironmonger, and on his demise, along with his brother, took over the same. On retirement of his brother, deceased took sole control of the present flourishing business, and his term of management covered about fifty years, he retiring in 1893, when two of his sons succeeded him.'

The view along Thorne Road.

Prior to the opening of the 'New Bridge' in 1910, the Bentley trams, when they needed repairs, were towed by a steam roller over the Great Northern Railway Company's level crossing, to the Greyfriars Road Depot. This picture was taken by the local photographer, Luke Bagshaw, shortly before the wiring for tram operations across the 'New Bridge' was completed. It also shows the original tram terminus in Marsh Gate.

Branson Street – the short entrance to Waterdale from Hall Gate/South Parade/Thorne Road.

Waterdale, looking towards the Trinity Presbyterian Church. Waterdale, or Weterdale as it was sometimes known, may be traced back to a deed of 1535. It is unclear when the road was put through, though it was extant on a map of 1769. During 1814 Waterdale became a venue for horse sales, and the name Horse Fair became attached to the area. Harwood Terrace on the left (named after Mathias Harwood), was built in around 1826. In 1882, the name Horse Fair was dropped in favour of a return to 'Waterdale.'

Cleveland Street with the Wood Street junction to the far left. A Salvation Army hut may be seen in the centre of the picture, with part of an area once known as High Street Buildings to the right. Cleveland Street was opened as a thoroughfare in 1833-34, having been named by the Town Clerk, Frederick Fisher, on 1 August 1831, in honour of William Henry Vane, who became Marquis of Cleveland in 1827 and Duke in 1833.

two

Shops

Left: Dolphin Chambers, Market Place, the former site of the Dolphin Inn which existed from at least 1781 until around 1892. Note the dolphins on each side at the top of the premises. Renowned local architects, Athron & Beck, occupied the first floor of the building, and Herbert Athron was noted as buying the premises in 1892. The Bijou cinema was formerly housed in a building at the rear.

Below: Blamires' shop on Beckett Road, with the notice in the window announcing that the premises had been extended. The business was established by Herbert Blamires in around 1922 and in later years shops were added in Cleveland Street as well as Huddersfield, Barnsley and Sheffield. After the Second World War only the one in Beckett Road was retained. Herbert died in 1956 and his son Robert continued the business until his own death in 1972. Robert's widow, Brenda, was at the helm from the time of her husband's death until 1978.

Above: Commercial premises on Cleveland Street, seen from the Wood Street junction. Featured are the premises of Brewitt & Son (shop fitters and undertakers) and Gray & Raynes (motor cycle and cycle dealers who also sold wirelesses). A sign in Gray & Raynes' window informs that 'guaranteed' cycles may be purchased from as little as £4 19s 6d.
Below: See the next page for caption.

Previous page: Prior to the First World War, T. Duckitt and Jack Chappell worked in a fish shop at 91 St Sepulchre Gate, which was owned and occupied by a Mrs Claybourne and her son. When the war broke out, Duckitt joined the Army, while Chappell went to work on munitions in the Plant Works. After the cessation of hostilities, Duckitt returned to the fish shop while Chappell went hawking around the local villages with a horse-and-dray. In 1934 the two men went into partnership in the shop. It was said the main attraction on the premises was a sturgeon, caught in the river Don at Kirk Bramwith during the early 1900s by a farmer with a hay fork. The sturgeon's first home was a Barnby Dun pub, where it was on show in a stable. Mr Claybourne bought the fish and had it preserved by a taxidermist. Mr Chappell's eldest son, Eric, helped in the shop. J. Chappell came out of the shop during March 1960, but carried on with stalls in the fish market. He died in 1971. The shop is no longer there.

The Claybourn business began at Askern when a bicycle and motor cycle repair shop was opened by Jack Ernest Claybourn, *c.* 1918. About four years later, he established a motor-garage on Askern's Doncaster Road. The business went from strength to strength and he gradually took over buildings in Hall Gate, Doncaster, finally acquiring them in 1931 when the car showrooms originally held four vehicles. Eventually, he owned the whole property and in the early days had the agency for Armstrong Siddely, Morrison Electric, Jowitt and Lanchester. From the 1960s, they dealt in Singer, Hillman Humber, Sunbeam, Austin, Morris, Daimler and Riley. A service department was established in 1963, but seven years later it moved to new larger premises near the Balby Bridge roundabout. At the same time the Hall Gate property was closed and the sales side of the business was concentrated in Prince's Street. This continued until 1978 when the new car showrooms were erected at Balby Bridge. When this occurred the Prince's Street premises were vacated and the entire Claybourn operation was concentrated at Balby. In 1987, Graham Claybourn, the founder's son, sold the business.

An interior view of Claybourn's Waterdale premises. A notice on the vehicle in the foreground announces: 'Singer Nine Sports Coupe 1934 model, the car that is setting the pace, £199, ex-works.'

Another interior view of Claybourn's Waterdale premises.

Claybourn's Waterdale premises.

Above: Butler's ironmongers store at the Silver Street/East Laith Gate junction. In John Butler's obituary, which was published in the *Doncaster Evening Post* of 16 January 1981, it was stated that the eighty-nine-year-old had taken a risk when he was aged twenty-one by starting a small ironmongery shop at 9 Silver Street. His gamble paid off, as soon the shop was too small and he moved a short distance down the street into a larger shop. The shop was closed on 15 January 1981, while eight of the twelve members of staff attended his funeral in Bridlington. He began as an apprentice ironmonger at an old shop called Charles Bros in Baxter Gate and, allegedly, believed in good old-fashioned personal service. His good friend, Managing Director Roy Smithson, who had worked at the shop for thirty-five years said: 'He believed in personal service and I will carry on in the same traditional ways.' Mr Butler's daughter, Barbara, who lived in Florida, was to take over ownership, but Mr Smithson was to carry on the running of the shop. Mr Butler, whose wife Helen had predeceased him by about ten years, had retired to Bridlington about twenty years earlier. At first he came to Doncaster on the train twice a week to cast an eye over the running of the shop and later motored over to the shop each week. Mr Butler lived in Town Moor Avenue before he moved to Bridlington. Butler's was always respected for its vast and varied stock where customers could buy almost everything, for John Butler could not resist a bargain. What Butler saw, Butler would buy, provided the price was right, and he would tour sales and Government auctions, particularly for ex-war department items. Often he would buy huge quantities, which would then remain in their original packaging, stacked from floor to ceiling in a bewildering catacomb of rooms, some still clothed in the stippled wallpaper of their original domestic days.

Opposite above: A row of properties extending between Spring Gardens and Duke Street on the north side of Cleveland Street. The Spring Gardens Methodist Chapel may be seen on the left. All the properties, including the chapel, were demolished during the 1960s. Amongst the traders shown here are the Home Wash (E.J. Barsby), Downs & Sons – butchers, and C. Rhodes – cycles. Note the sign on the right stating: 'Man you've earned that Guiness.'

Right: Davies & Balmforth's premises at the Market Place/Scot Lane junction

Below: W. Delanoy's leather works at 32 Baxter Gate.

Above: Dewhurst the coach builder's premises on Cleveland Street.

Left: The Marks & Spencer emporium in Baxter Gate. The company established itself in Doncaster during the 1920s and its premises were extended through to French Gate during the early 1960s.

Opposite below: The junction of Harwood Terrace, Waterdale and Wood Street. Featured prominently is Fisher's corner café, boasting prominently that it could accommodate 200 customers. Note the Doncaster Corporation bus bound for Rossington on the left and the London-Leeds bus on the right. By the 1920s the area in front of Harwood Terrace was being used as a bus station.

Above: A row of properties awaiting demolition on the south side of Cleveland Street during the early 1960s. They include the business premises of R. Elliff, photographic materials and W. Maw, florist and fruiterer. Reg Elliff was born in 1909 and started his photography business in Balby before moving to larger premises at 89 Cleveland Street, seen here during the 1950s. Redevelopment in Cleveland Street during the 1960s meant Reg and his son Ken, who had joined the business, had to find alternative business premises. They finally decided on a Denaby chapel, existing there until recent times. Reg Elliff died in 1975.

Left: Property on the north side of Silver Street before street widening took place in the area during the early part of the twentieth century. The business premises featured include a confectioner and the butcher
P. Lund (on the right).

Below: The Grand Clothing Hall in the Market Place. The Albany Temperance Hotel is on the right.

Opposite below: Hopkinson Bros business premises on Cleveland Street, selling cycles, washing and wringing machines. A notice in the window advertises Frister & Rossman's sewing machines.

Above: At a special meeting of the shareholders of Killengrey & Co. Ltd, manufacturers of butterscotch and other sweetmeats in French Gate, held at the works on Saturday 30 November 1901, it was decided that they should go into voluntary liquidation because of failing business. The business was started in a small way during the mid-nineteenth century by J. Killengrey, with manufacturing premises in Silver Street and French Gate. During the 1890s, the firm employed around 100 hands, turning out 15 to 20 tons of 'spice' each week. Butterscotch and rock were the two main sweetmeats. In 1866, when the Prince of Wales was a guest at the Doncaster Races, the firm presented him with an elaborate box of their butterscotch. It was graciously accepted and permission was given to them to use the term 'Royal'. Around 1870, J. Hastie married one of J. Killengrey's daughters and afterwards assisted his father-in-law in the business. He later purchased the whole concern, but retained the old style of the firm. In subsequent years, Killengrey's old site in French Gate (pictured here) was acquired by garage owner W. Jackson and redeveloped.

A vehicle belonging to the Model Dairy in Netherhall Road.

L. Parker outside his newsagent and tobacconist shop at 74 Cemetery Road.

Archibald Ramsden's premises, which sold pianos and organs.

The frontage of Dennis Roberts' shop in St Sepulchre Gate. Dennis Roberts died in 1896 and his son, Walter, subsequently ran the business with partners and family members for some time afterwards. Walter Roberts died in 1923 and four years later the company ceased trading in St Sepulchre Gate, as the Corporation required the premises for street widening. One of the firm's directors, Donald Boulter, opened new premises at 11-13 Scot Lane, under the style of Dennis Roberts & Co. This, however, was only short lived and the name of Dennis Roberts, synonymous with drapery in the town for more than a century, faded away. Today, Burtons currently trade on part of Dennis Roberts' old St Sepulchre Gate site.

Timber merchant C.E. Roelich's business premises in Union Street.

Alfred Sanderson, the son of a London hotel proprietor, was only eleven years old when his father died and he was adopted by a Mrs Hall of the Old George Hotel, Doncaster, his aunt on his father's side. In 1857 he went to Leeds, where he became an apprentice at a grocery business, and in 1860 came back to Doncaster as an assistant with Thomas Parkinson, in premises at the St Sepulchre Gate/Printing Office Street corner, which is pictured here. When Parkinson retired in 1873, Sanderson was offered the business and took it over with the late Jospeh Stringer and John West. The latter left the business ten years later, and it was carried on for some years on that corner site, and at No. 10 St Sepulchre Gate (on the French Gate side and near Clock Corner). But, the former shop was eventually given up. The partnership between Sanderson and Stringer was, in time, dissolved, and Sanderson went into partnership his son Theo. The firm then became Sanderson & Son. The business was carried on for a long time at both Nos 8 and 10 St Sepulchre Gate, the former being the provision department. Owing to the shortage of assistants during the First World War, the provision department was given up. Not long after Alfred Sanderson's death in March 1924, within a few weeks of his eighty-first birthday, the business premises at No. 10 St Sepulchre Gate were sold for £12,700 to Messrs Stead & Simpson, the well-known boot and shoe manufacturers.

John Steadman was born in Mattersey and around 1877 established himself as a horsebreaker in Silver Street. He soon extended his business and again moved, this time to premises in Highfield Road. And he became a very well known figure on the box of his four in hand. Drives to the Dukeries and other spots of interest became his speciality. With the arrival of the taxi-cab, the four in hand days rapidly became a mere memory, and those of the horse cab were numbered. Steadman was not slow to take steps to keep abreast of the times. New premises in Cleveland Street, seen here, were acquired and opened in 1909, as a garage and a taxi office. John Steadman died in 1922 and the Cleveland Street premises were vacated in 1963 when the firm moved to Balby. Hodgson Holdings took control of the company in 1987.

Frederick Swaby, a fish and game dealer, died at the early age of fifty-four on Friday 2 November 1928. Frederick was a son of Robert Swaby and a grandson of Samuel Plumpton Swaby, who came to Doncaster from North Somercotes Lincolnshire, during the nineteenth century. He started a fish and game business in the High Street, seen here near the Ram Hotel. The business was afterwards successfully conducted by one of his sons. It was later merged into one in St Sepulchre Gate and was carried on by W.C. Burkinshaw.

Left: Swaby's shop on a site subsequently taken by the Danum Hotel.

Below: A line of Westfields removal vehicles with the Don Cinema at Bentley providing a backdrop.

three

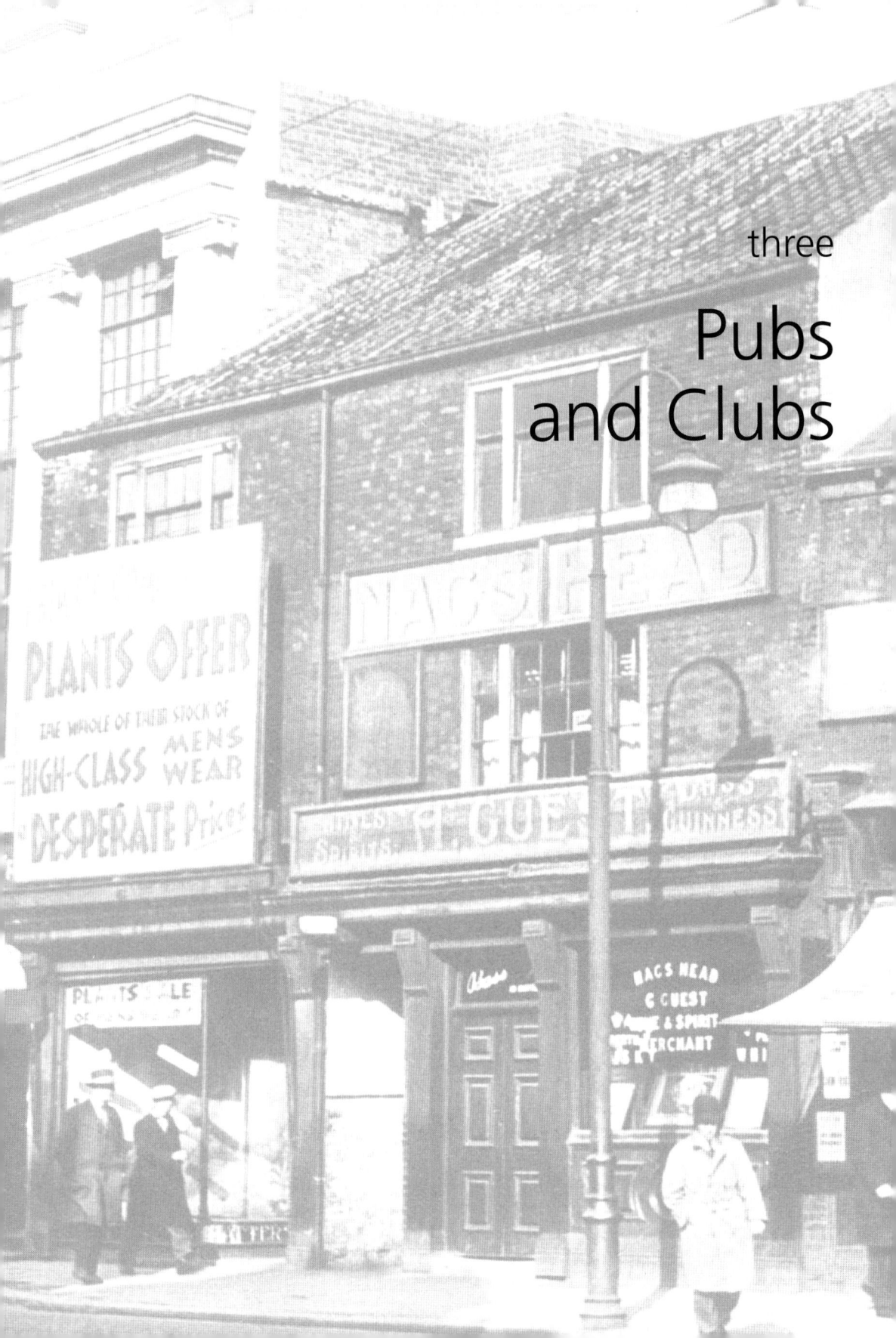

Pubs
and Clubs

Beethams or the George & Dragon Vaults at the St George Gate/Baxter Gate corner. The pub dates from at least 1787 and was rebuilt in around 1871, and again in 1964. Past owners have included the Beetham family and Richard Whitaker & Sons Ltd. The premises once held a six day licence (closed on Sundays).

A view card of the Danum Hotel which occupies the former site of the Ram Hotel. During November 1907 it was announced that the Ram Hotel at the Cleveland Street/High Street corner had been sold to the Sheffield grocers Messrs Greensmith for £4,500. Later, the Doncaster Corporation gave £4,600 for the property, but they had an ulterior motive. The property needed to be pulled down for the existing road at that end of Cleveland Street to be widened from 30ft to 42ft, with as much as 12ft being taken off in some places. The corner was also to be rounded off, and the pub's old billiard room was to disappear. At the time, the *Sheffield Telegraph* mentioned that towards the close of the eighteenth century, the hotel was known as the Bay Horse.

During early March 1975, it was announced that the Elephant Hotel, St Sepulchre Gate, which had closed the previous year, was likely to be demolished. At a meeting of the DMBC technical services committee, an outline planning permission for the demolition and the redevelopment of the site as a three-storey branch bank was given to the Yorkshire Bank Ltd. A few members of the committee fought a rear guard action in a bid to save the sixty-year-old building, but others were anxious to see it go. 'I don't think it is necessary to demolish the front,' said Cllr Stanley Wilson, '...it could be changed for banking use while still preserving most of the façade.' But Cllr Rowland Williamson claimed the frontage had already been destroyed. Since Hardy's the furniture firm had taken it over, the building had become an 'absolute disgrace,' he said and posters are seen here plastered over the whole frontage.

Right: Property on the south side of St Sepulchre Gate just before demolition took place in order to facilitate street widening. The buildings depicted include Plants, a men's clothier and the Nags Head public house. The *Doncaster Chronicle* of 8 February 1934 gives the following information on the Plants: 'The history of the firm of Messrs Plant & Sons, Baxter Gate, French Gate and St Sepulchre Gate goes back well over 100 years, starting with the present T.W. Plant's grandfather, who had a gentlemen's hat shop in Worksop in 1800. He had a family of ten sons, all of whom took up similar lines of business. One Mr W.C. Plant came to Doncaster and opened a shop near the Clock end of High street. This was the beginning of a business concern which has prospered with years.' Following rebuilding, the Nags Head presented an impressive Art Deco appearance to the street line.

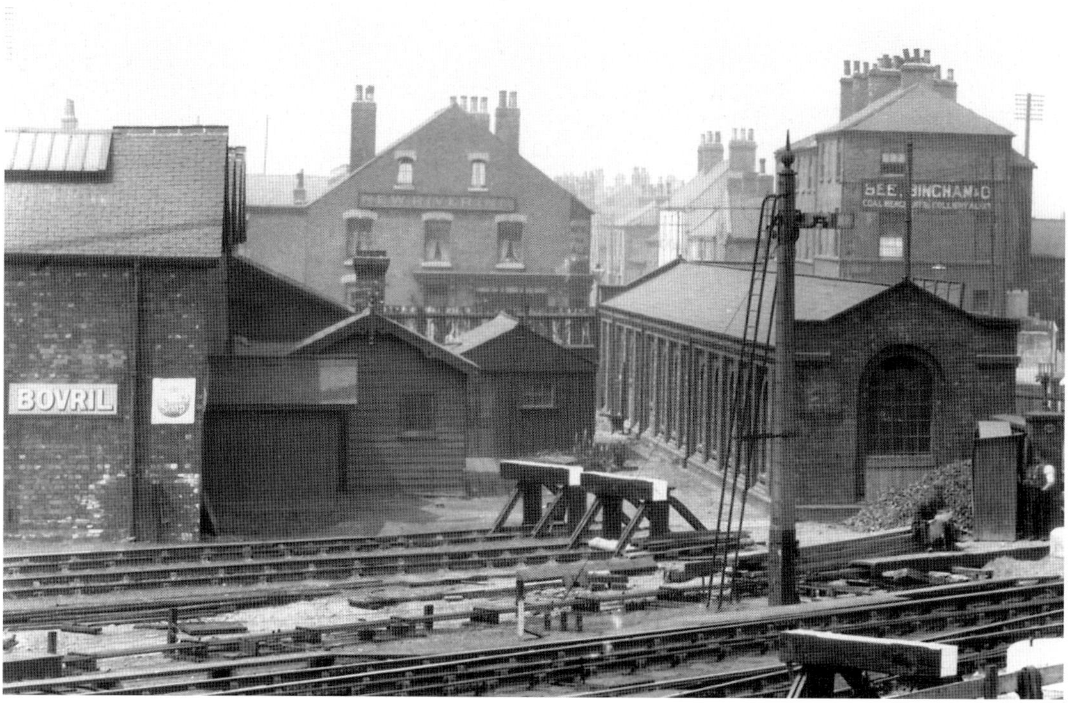
BOVRIL

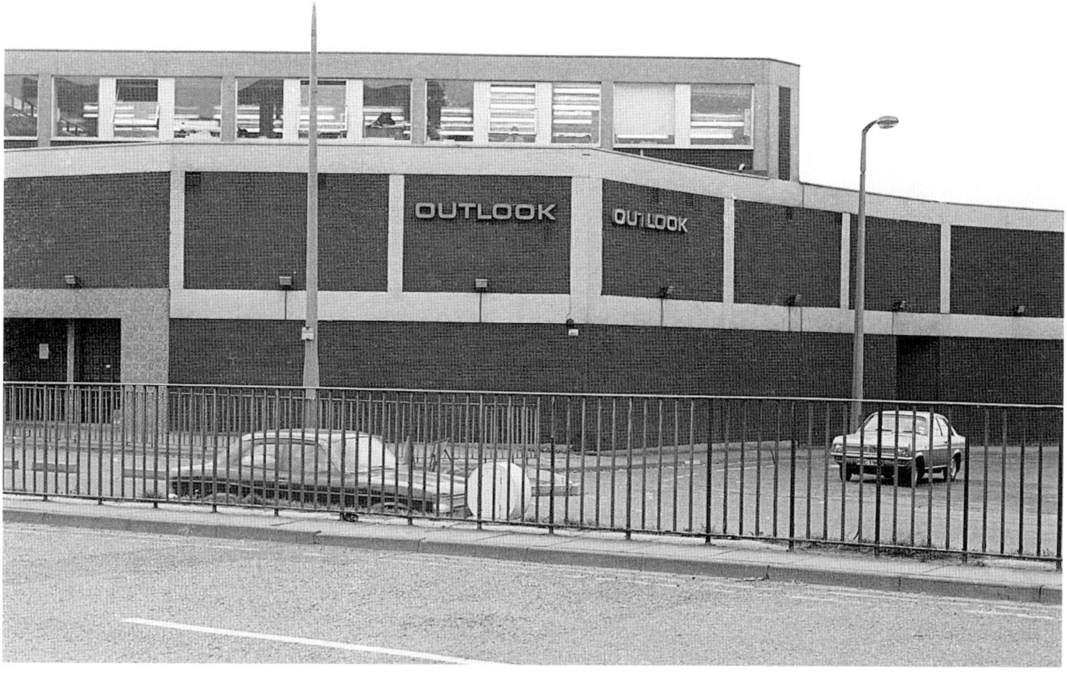
OUTLOOK
OUTLOOK

Above: Rotters' discotheque, Silver Street. Constructed in the 1960s, the premises began life as the Top Rank Suite. In subsequent years it has undergone several more name changes and refits.

Opposite above: In a view facing north along Marsh Gate, the New River Tavern may be seen in the centre, during the construction of North Bridge. The New River Tavern dated from at least the early 1850s and was extant until 1937. The inn probably took its name from the nearby canal, which was cut in 1842. Past owners of the premises included the River Dun Company, Nicholson Bros and Whitworth, Son & Nephew.

Opposite below: The Outlook nightclub on Trafford Way. During the 1970s it became a much-loved venue for New Wave and Punk bands. Those appearing there included Siouxsie and the Banshees, the Sex Pistols, X-ray Specs and the Rich Kids. The building has since been demolished.

The Saracen's Head public house on the north side of Cleveland Street with the Old Exchange Brewery Tavern adjacent on the left. The Saracen's Head dates from at least 1826, and the Tavern from around 1867. The latter was converted, along with the extensive brewery at the rear, to temporary office accommodation in 1946 by the Doncaster Corporation. The Tavern itself was demolished in 1982.

The Staff of Life at the Whittaker Street/Young Street corner. The inn, which dates from at least 1862, was partly covered with vitrolite in the mid-1930s. It was rebuilt in around 1967, almost on the original site, as part of the Golden Acres development.

Above: The Star Inn at the St James Street/Cemetery Road corner, looking towards the town centre. The inn which could be traced back to 1822, was rebuilt in 1914 and closed on 17 October 1971.

Left: Zhivagos discotheque in Silver Street.

The Three Legs in St Sepulchre Gate could trace its history back to around 1782. It was rebuilt in around 1913 as part of the St Sepulchre Gate widening scheme, renamed the Yorkist in 1969 and closed during 1984.

four
Buildings

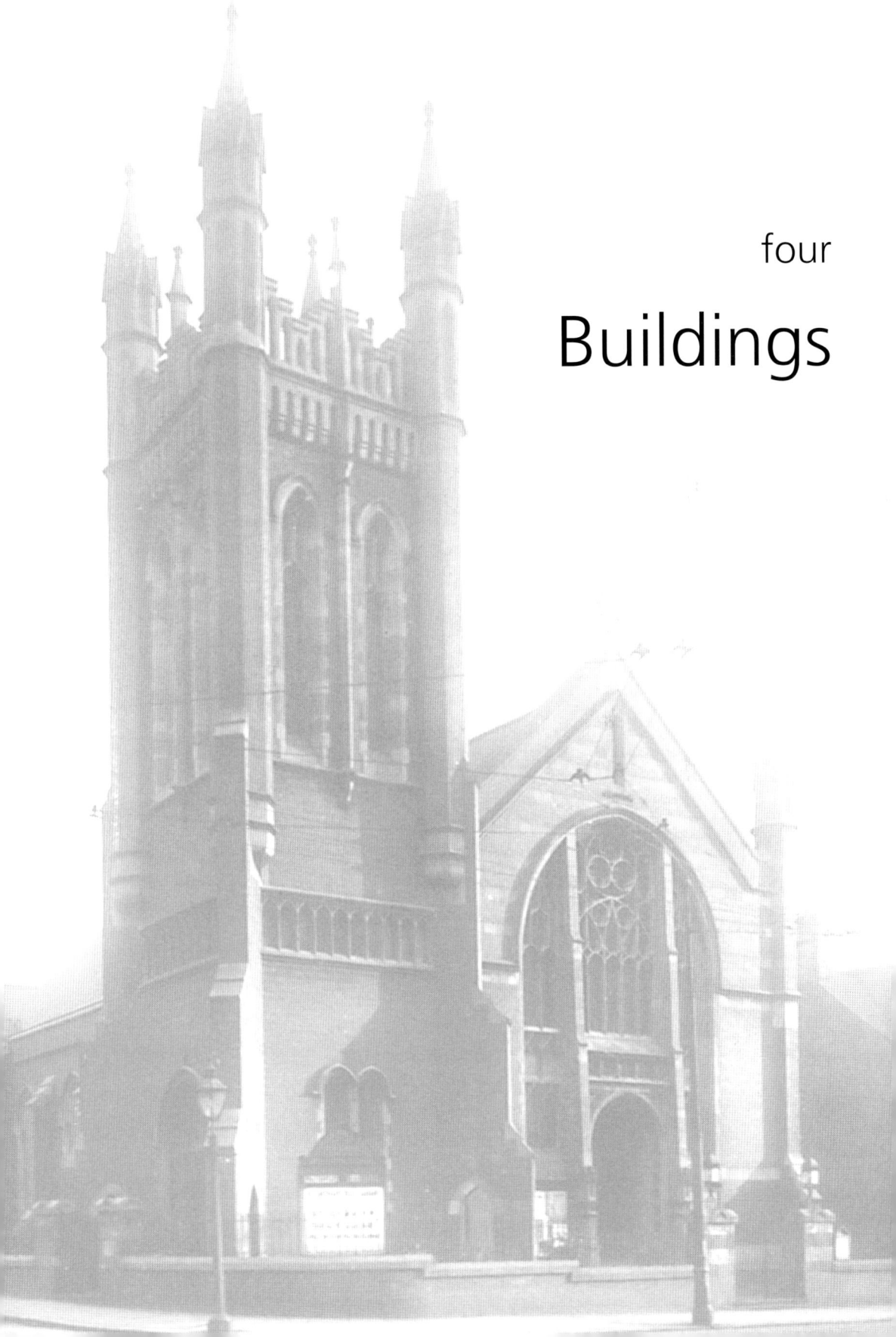

Above: Interior view of the NatWest Bank in High Street. The bank, designed by Walter Brierley, opened on 30 April 1928. In the Civic Trust Newsletter, written in April 1988, Eric Braim states: 'The handsome classical elevation accords well with the Mansion House which it reflects in its round headed windows... However the chief glory of the building is its magnificent banking hall which is double cube...and was considered by Inigo Jones, the great Renaissance architect to be an ideal proportion.'

Left: The Netherhall Road Methodist Chapel with the school church to the left. Netherhall Road extends to the right, Highfield Road to the left and Broxholme Lane cuts through the centre. The building contract for the Nether Hall Road Chapel, described as being sixteenth-century Gothic in style, was £5,800, with the seating being able to accommodate 750 members of the congregation. G.F. Morris in his *Churches and Chapels of Old Doncaster* states: 'In 1903 the [Wesleyan Methodists] opened a splendid-looking chapel in Nether Hall Road... As late as the 1950s the chapel had annual performances of the Messiah with a choir of over a hundred and top professional singers like Isobel Baillie and Kathleen Ferrier came as soloists.'

The Arcadia in Waterdale began life as a concert pavilion on Whit Monday June 1922. It was promoted by Henry Russell, built by Swift Bros and Haslam Ltd, could seat 800 people in tip-up seats and was furnished by Sheard Binnington. One of the managers was Fred Ingleby. Doncaster Corporation bought the premises for £8,500 in 1948, and a year later after renovations, it reopened as the Arts Centre. It has since been renamed Civic Theatre.

A new skating rink behind South Parade, Doncaster, was opened to the public on Monday 15 August 1909. The work, which was the outcome of local enterprise, was completed rapidly, giving skaters of Doncaster a large and handsome hall devoted to what was then a new cult. The rink was a red brick building, with a girded roof about 30ft high, and provided 14,000ft of skating area. The skating hall was 200ft long and over 70ft wide. Skaters had a clear run down the rink's sides of nearly 70 yards, which compared favourably with the very best rinks. There was a 10ft promenade all around the skating area, separate cloak and skate rooms for males and females, a band in a gallery and a refreshment buffet on the ground floor. How the venture fared in subsequent years is described by Peter Coote in The Salutation Inn (1991):

'The venture was only successful for a short period and by 1914 the rink was leased for use as Government offices. They had moved out by 1925 and in their place a military presence soon became established. For many years, until its demolition about twenty years ago, the building was known as Scarborough Barracks.'

Above: Spring Gardens Methodist Chapel, at the Spring Gardens/Cleveland Street junction, was built in 1804 and enlarged sixteen years later. Adjoining the building was a superintendent minister's house. Edward Miller, in his *History and Antiquities of Doncaster and its Vicinity* (1804), stated that the building was 'handsome and judiciously contrived for the congregation distinctly to hear the preacher.' The chapel survived until the 1960s when it was demolished for redevelopment in the area.

Left: The old water wheel and engine house erected over the river Cheswold in the early eighteenth century for the supply of water to the public. Both were situated on part of a site later taken for the erection of the Northern Bus Station. The flow of water from the wheel is adequately described by Colin Walton in his *Changing Face of Doncaster* (1980):'The water was forced through the principal pipes in a southerly direction from the wheel in French Gate, through High Street to the summit of Hall Gate, where there was a reservoir capable of holding 28,000 gallons... there were also branch mains for supplying the east and west sides of the town.'

five

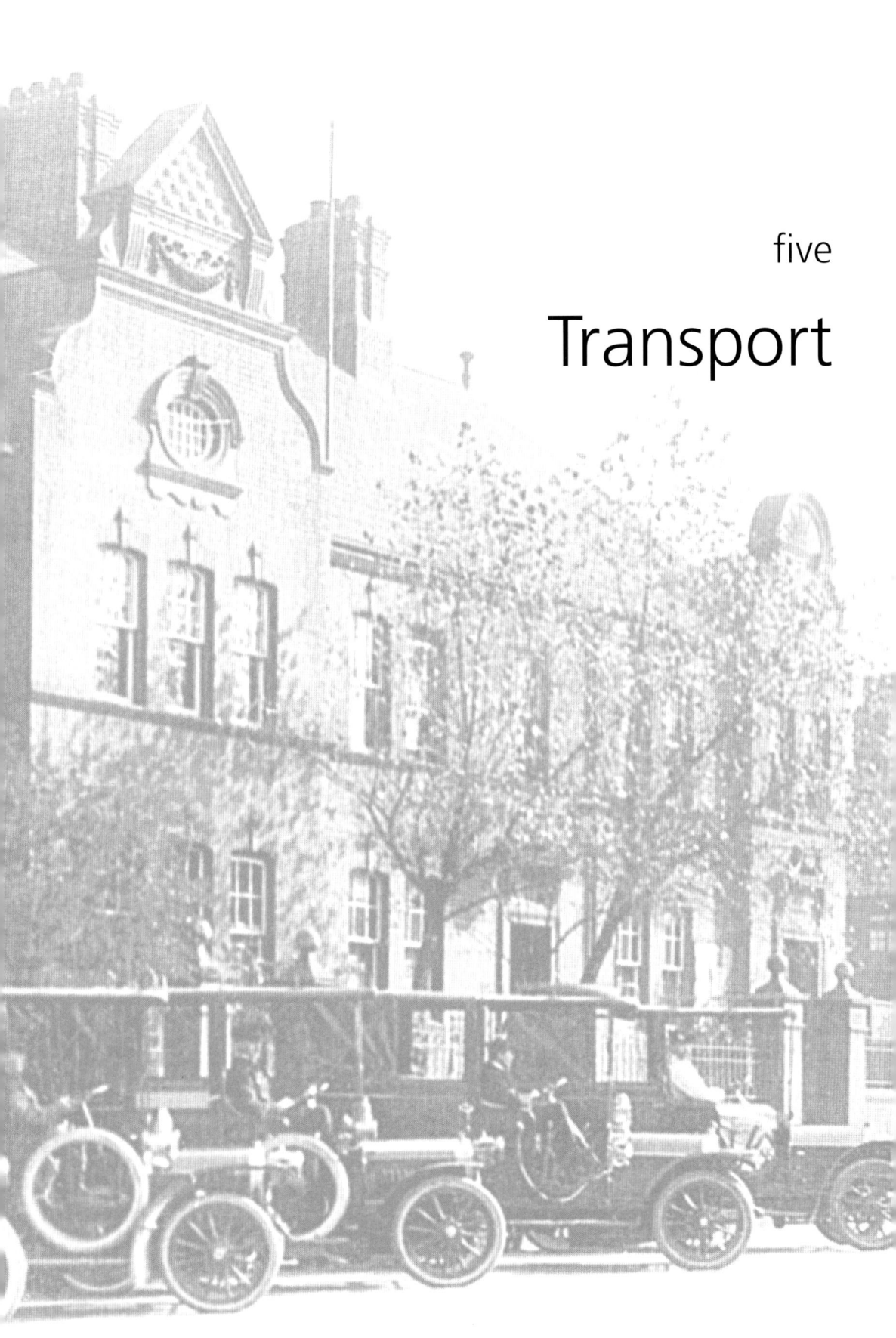

Transport

Above: Trams ceased to run on the Beckett Road route in 1929 and were replaced by trolley buses. Initially the trolley service terminated at the junction with Wentworth Road, but was later extended. A Beckett Road trolleybus is seen here on 1 April 1954, passing the Broxholme Lane/Copley Road junction whilst making an outward journey. Dating from 1945, Sunbeam WD/D trolley No. 391 was one of a batch of ex-Southend-on-Sea vehicles acquired by Doncaster Transport in 1954. It was rebodied in 1958 and withdrawn in 1962.

Opposite: Two views of a decorated open-top tram near the Grey Friars Road Depot. The vehicle plays a part in the town's peace celebrations.

63

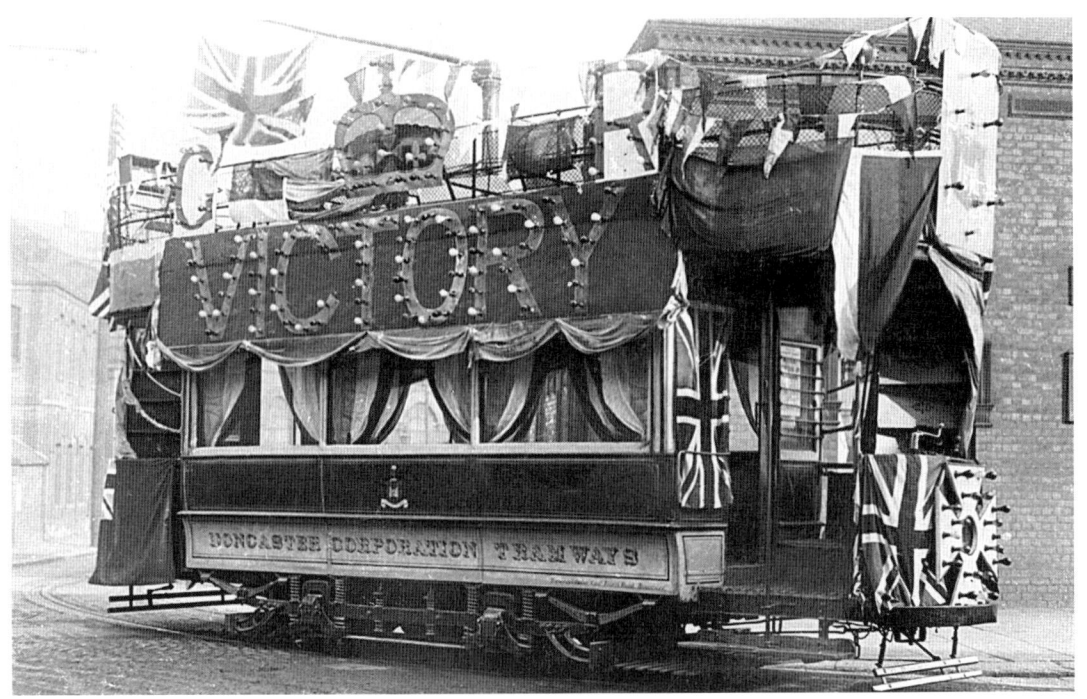

Above: A busy scene in West Laith Gate, the town centre terminus for the Hexthorpe and Balby Trolleys. Services on these routes began during 1929 and 1931 respectively. The Balby route became the busiest trolleybus service. Six vehicles usually operated on the route during weekdays, with ten on Saturdays. On the right is the rear entrance to the Bull's Head public house.

Left: A motorwoman at the helm of car No. 13. During the First World War, as large numbers of the male population joined the fighting abroad, women became employed for the first time in a variety of jobs, including both tram driving and conducting. In Doncaster during this period the trams were staffed almost entirely by women. Car No. 13 came to Doncaster in a batch of fifteen made by Dick Kerr in 1902. Nos 10-15 were fitted with top deck covers, and direct staircases, by Dick Kerr in 1913 and also becoming balcony cars. Nos 6-15 were withdrawn in 1930.

Trolleybus No. 351 on its way to the town centre depot in Grey Friars Road. Note Hanley's mill in the background. Travelling via the Market Place, High Fisher Gate and Grey Friars Road provided an alternative route to and from the Depot, instead of the one via French Gate.

In this view from North Bridge facing the town centre, the Bentley town centre terminus is on the left. A trolleys turned round at the terminus by utilising a 'turning circle,' as demonstrated by the unidentified vehicles in the photograph.

Opposite: Two views of Smith & Sons fleet on taxis. The picture opposite above was taken in Waterdale, the one below it was near Station Road. The firm of Smith & Son, motor engineers and bodybuilders, which once had premises extending from St Sepulchre Gate through to West Laith Gate, was established by George Smith in 1805. Under the control of successive generations of sons, it flourished until it became one of the best known coach building businesses in the country, employing a large number of men. Their interests extended to Sheffield and Retford and even as far afield as Johannesburg, where the branch was managed by one of George's great-grandsons. The firm built the coach used by the High Sheriffs of Yorkshire. The firm also earned a reputation for its carriage horses and, whenever royalty visited Doncaster, Smith & Son provided the horses, and in some cases the carriages too. With the advent of the motor car, the firm adapted their business and works to the changing needs of the time. As the coach building business declined, there was an expansion in the business dealing with motor car body building, motor engineering and the sale of motor vehicles of all kinds. From time to time the St Sepulchre Gate premises were enlarged until, on the formation of a limited liability company in 1922, it was necessary to move to more commodious premises in Hall Gate and Waterdale.

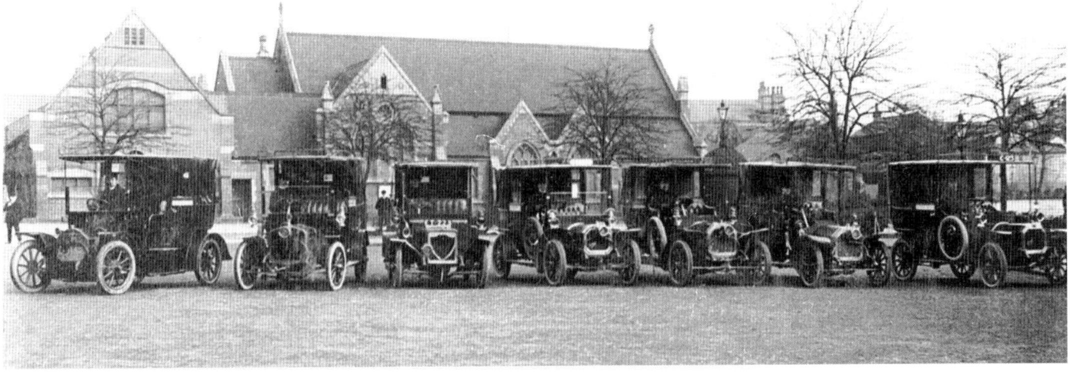

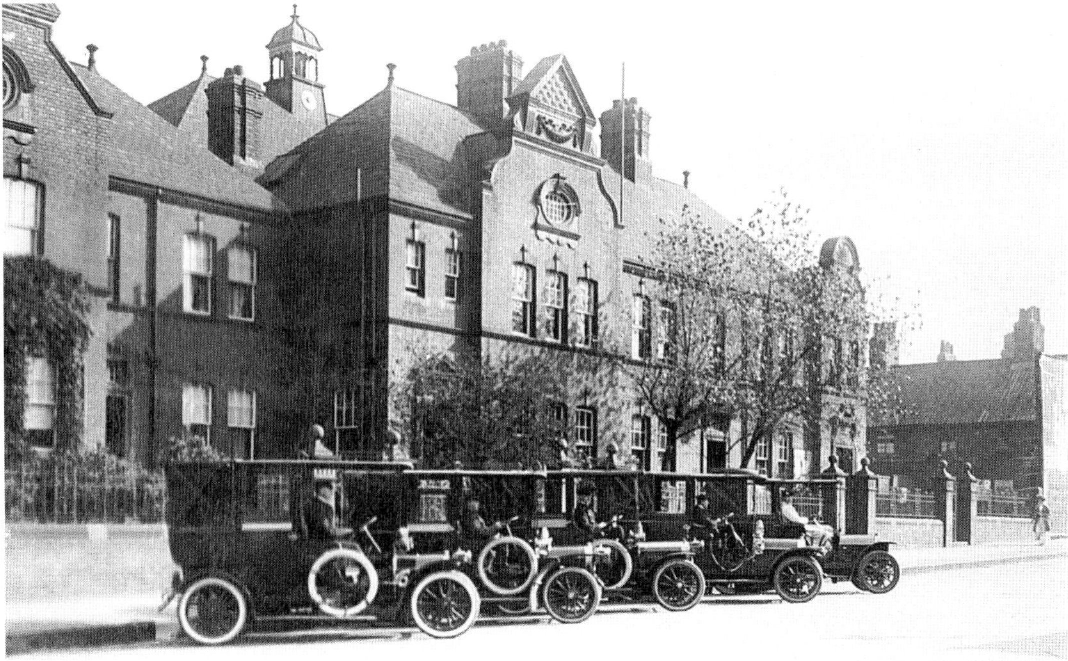

Spring Gardens looking towards the Good Woman Café on St Sepulchre Gate. The Golden Ball public house is on the right. Note the bow windows and wrought iron balconies on some of the properties on the left. Rebodied 1943 Sunbeam W D/D trolleybus No. 396, is pictured near where the Southern Bus Station now stands. The vehicle was purchased from the Mexborough & Swinton Traction Company in 1955 when it was surplus to requirements.

Part of the St Sepulchre Gate section of the Hexthorpe trolley route, with the YMCA in the background. The outward and return journeys on the Hexthorpe trolley route were only supposed to take ten minutes each.

Left: Tram staff, a motorman and conductor, pose for the camera alongside a vehicle. In the early days of tram operations, thirty-five drivers and conductors were employed and they each worked fifty-four hours per week. A driver earned a maximum wage of £1 7s 0d, whilst a conductor received £1 2s 6d.

Below: A Beckett Road trolley in St Sepulchre Gate, about to begin an outward journey. The town's last trolley service operated on the Beckett Road route on 14 December 1963. Noticeable on the left is an effigy of an elephant outside the Elephant Hotel.

Trolleybus No. 27, operating on a race 'special'. Although both the Hyde Park and Racecourse 'circular' trolleybus routes were capable of taking passengers to and from the Racecourse, trolleybuses were operated around the 'circle' in the Hyde Park direction only during the town's celebrated Race Week. This method was considered to be the best way for the trolleybuses to cope with the many thousands of people visiting the event each year.

A murky day and a Beckett Road trolley waits before crossing from Printing Office Street to the town centre terminus along St Sepulchre Gate.

six

Events

Above: A scene at the 1934 carnival display, where Messer & Fullard won 2nd prize.

Opposite: On Wednesday 3 July 1912, Prince Arthur of Connaught visited the Royal Showground at Doncaster. At the railway station, elaborate arrangements were made for the arrival of the Prince. In the station yard, by about half past twelve, the guard of honour and the mounted escort were drawn up to accompany his Royal highness to the Show Ground. As the Prince emerged from the station, the Territorials were brought smartly to a salute while the band struck up the national anthem. His Royal Highness was conducted to the lines of the Guard of Honour, walking with Captain Parkin. When the inspection was completed, the party entered the carriages that were to convey them to the Show Ground, with the High Sheriff riding in the splendid official coach with a coachman and footman on the box. The procession was headed by the new Chief Constable (Mr W. Adams) and the coach carrying the Prince included his equerry and the mayor. The ceremony of the royal visit to the Show Ground was impressive though somewhat formal. The Prince drove straight up to the Royal Pavilion, where he was met on the steps by Lord Middleton and other members and officials of the Society. Outside the Royal Pavilion, a large crowd had gathered. The band of the Queen's Own Yorkshire Dragoons, stationed near the Royal Pavilion, played the National Anthem as the Prince drove up. After lunch the Prince showed great interest in the work done by children and afterwards he went round the side of the Show Yard to see the exhibition of the Canadian Government. Tea was served in the Royal Pavilion, after which the Prince left the ground to catch his train – the 6.30 from Doncaster to King's Cross.

The Prince's Equerry. Prince Arthur. The Hon Rupert Beckett. The High Sheriff of

Visit Of Prince Arthur Of Connaught To Royal Show, Doncaster, July 2 1912.

The Prince Inspects Guard of Honour. 28.

Members of the Doncaster Corporation form part of a procession in Baxter Gate.

Peace celebrations in Bridge Street, Hexthorpe (now demolished), 1945.

Left: The visit of HRH Princess Christian to the Wood Street Infirmary on 26 April 1906. Gary Swann, in *The Doncaster Royal Infirmary 1792-1972*, states:

'She was met on the steps of the building by Dr Christy Wilson, who introduced Sister Florence and the nursing staff. After touring the wards and the new extensions, where she met and talked to all the patients, the Princess signed some of the Infirmary books and before leaving intimated that she would be pleased to become the first royal patron of the institution.'

Below: The view down Camden Street towards St James' Schools on St Sepulchre Gate. It depicts passengers who are attending the Co-operative Society's gala on Burnett's field at Hexthorpe – they are boarding open-top and covered-top trams.

Above: A procession (purpose unknown) crosses from High Street into Hall Gate. This is probably the view from a balcony in Cuttriss' High Street premises. On the right is the Ram Hotel and Dowson's premises are adjacent.

Below: The Fancy Dress Cycle Parade, with members of the local fire brigade in the foreground on 1 August 1910.

Above and below: Tank Bank Week began in Doncaster on Monday 23 April 1918. The tank, 'Egbert', was uncovered on Sunday afternoon in the GNR Goods Yard in St Sepulchre Gate. It went to the Racecourse along with soldiers with fixed bayonets and a guard of the Doncaster Battalion of the West Riding Volunteers. The curiosity stimulated by the tank was tremendous. People travelled for miles to gaze at it. During the progress of the tank along Bennetthorpe (seen here in one of the pictures), and during the demonstration, an aviator constantly circled over the huge crowds, swooped down and dropped sheets of leaflets containing directions of how to invest etc. The Market Square (seen in the second picture) had flags and bunting. The Mayor opened the event, saying Doncaster had done well in sending men to the front to fight and it was the town's duty to back up those men by subscribing to the War Savings to bring the war to a successful end. At the end of the campaign, a total of £410,000 was reached, which was more than most expected.

Marsh Gate, looking north in the floods of the 1930s. The main buildings in the picture include the George & Dragon public house on the left and P.D. Warriner's garage in the distance.

Floods in Marsh Gate, looking towards the town centre, in 1932. The George & Dragon is seen on the right this time.

Unfortunately no details may be found about this picture but some reader may hold the key to the mystery?

A procession passes the Mansion House in High Street, with vehicles from the tractor company – International Harvesters (later Case) – featuring prominently.

Another view of the procession seen on the previous page. A placard displayed by Doncaster's young farmers states: 'Farmers of Britain are hitting their target, are you?'

Participants in the Doncaster Infirmary Demonstration, on 6 May 1911

Above and below: A site for a new hospital which was to eventually replace the one in Whitaker Street was purchased from the Fitzwilliam estate at the junction of Thorne Road and Armthorpe Road. The foundation stone was laid by the Prince of Wales on 12 October 1926. The new infirmary on Thorne Road was ready to accept patients by June 1930. Initially it only had room for 150 in-patients. Lord Lonsdale officially opened the new building on 21 August 1935.

A curious scene at the Cleveland Street/Printing Office Street junction, showing the Doncaster intercepting sewer Shaft 16 headgear.

The arrival of King George and Queen Mary at Doncaster station on Monday 8 July 1912. The visit formed part of the royal couple's visit to South Yorkshire as they acquainted themselves with the lives, manner of work and homes of their industrial subjects. They arrived at Doncaster station to an enthusiastic reception. The itinerary included a visit to a miner's cottage at the Woodland's model village, the King's descent of Elsecar Colliery, and a tea party at Conisbrough Castle, before staying with Lord Fitzwilliam at Wentworth.

Market Place looking towards the Woolpack Hotel, where a large crowd gathered to listen to a speech and inspect the heavy artillery in the foreground.

Members of the Doncaster Motorcycle Club outside the Danum Hotel. In a short article headed 'Doncaster Club's Opening Run', the *Doncaster Chronicle* of 1 April 1910 states: 'The members of the new Doncaster and District Motor cycling Club had their opening spin on Good Friday. Starting in the morning they journeyed on the Great North Road to Newark, and on to Swinderby. Here an enjoyable dinner was partaken of at the Red Lion Hotel. The return was via Lincoln, Gainsbro, Haxey and Branton. The weather was glorious and the first run was a great success and much enjoyed.'

Doncaster Motorcycle Club members. Whether this was taken at the same time as the picture on the previous page is unclear.

Mrs Roelich's young dancing pupil's fancy dress party, which was held on 31 January 1920.

Mr and Mrs Roelich's fancy dress carnival, on 30 January 1935.

The interior of Oxford Place Infants School during the Peace Celebrations of 1919.

Left: The celebration of the Silver Jubilee of King George and Queen Mary in Oxford Street during May 1935. The *Doncaster Gazette* of 9 May 1935 had the following to say about Jubilee Day in the town: 'Doncaster too will remember how it celebrated the Silver Jubilee of our King and Queen, in laughter and in gaiety. For a time it forgot its cares and troubles and lived only for the day, revelling in the glorious sunshine that came in the early morning and never once lost its brilliance.'

Below: Looking towards the Nine Arch Hexthorpe Bridge, this possibly shows crowds waiting to catch a glimpse of King George VI and Queen Elizabeth on their visit to the town.

The stone-laying ceremony of the Free Christian Church's new lecture hall, between Wood Street and Hall Gate on 11 April 1912. The *Doncaster Chronicle*, published on the same day reported:

'The new building stands almost on the same site of the old Unitarian Church, and when completed and furnished, will have cost about £3,200. The architects are Messrs Dunn and Mendham of Birmingham and the contractors, Messrs C. Sprakes & Son of Doncaster. At present it is only proposed to build a lecture hall, a Sunday School and an Institute. The hall will, when completed, be used for church purposes until such time as funds allow the building of a church, when the premises facing Hall Gate will have to be pulled down, and the church built to front Hall Gate.'

A children's street party in South Street, Hyde Park, on Silver Jubilee Day, in 1935

The peace celebrations of 1919, possibly in South Street Hyde Park.

Infirmary Parade in Waterdale with Harwood Terrace to the left, *c.* 1912.

Peace celebrations in Wellington Street (now demolished), 1919.

Celebrations in Wellington Street on VJ Day.

Celebrations in Wellington Street on VJ Day.

Celebrations in Whitaker Street with Wood Street in the distance.

seven

Formal Groups

HM Queen Elizabeth in High Street whilst on a visit to the town in 1975.

Brass finishers at the Great Northern Railway's Plant Works at Hexthorpe.

Class 11 at the Council School, Chequer Road, 1924. H.R. Wormald in his *Modern Doncaster* (1973) states:

'The Corporation's Abstract of Accounts show that between 1903 and 1923 only £11,771 capital was spent on elementary education comprising the purchase of Stirling Street, new schools at Chequer Road Infants in 1903, and some slight alterations to Hyde Park Schools. The major part of the present Chequer Road (Beechfield) schools were constructed in 1926, costing £22,157.'

Class 13 at the Council School, Chequer Road, 1924.

Class 4 at the Council School, Chequer Road, 1924.

Class 7 at the Council School, Chequer Road, 1924.

Engine drivers at the rear of the Burns Tavern, Cemetery Road.

A gathering of children in Waterdale attending the Co-op Gala, c. 1910. Note the building work taking place in the background on the Municipal High School for Girls.

Opposite above: Members of Doncaster's Excelsior Minstrel Troupe.

Opposite below: Pupils at the Hyde Park (Corporation) School on Green Dyke Lane. The school was designed by the Borough Surveyor and opened by the Mayor on 26 September 1895, for 220 boys, 220 girls and 272 mixed infants. The cost was £5,700 and teaching began on 1 October 1895. The premises continued to be used as schools until the 1960s.

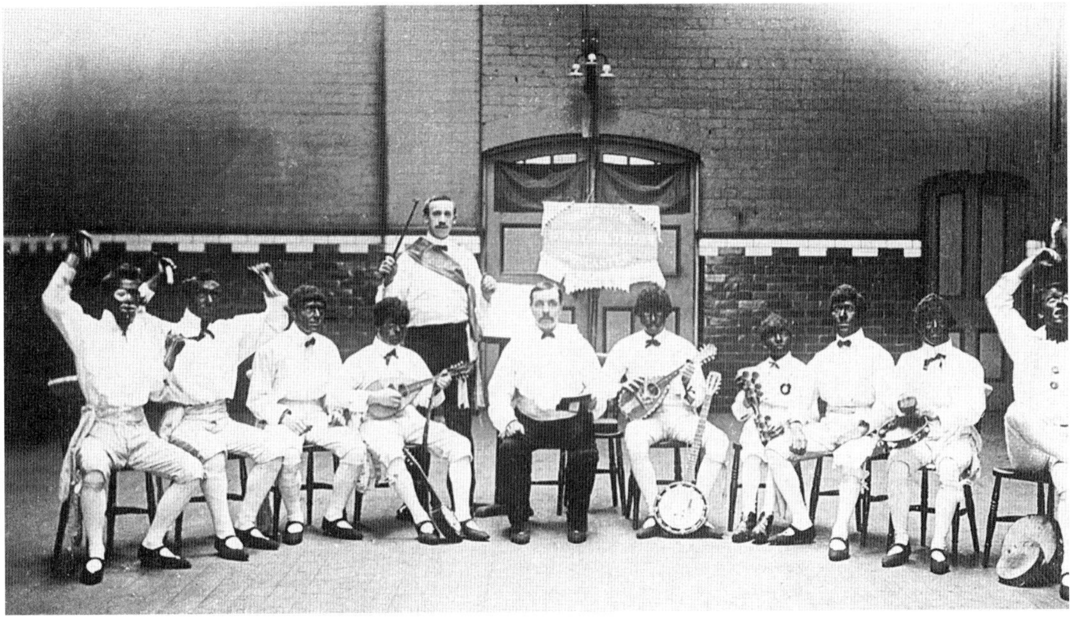

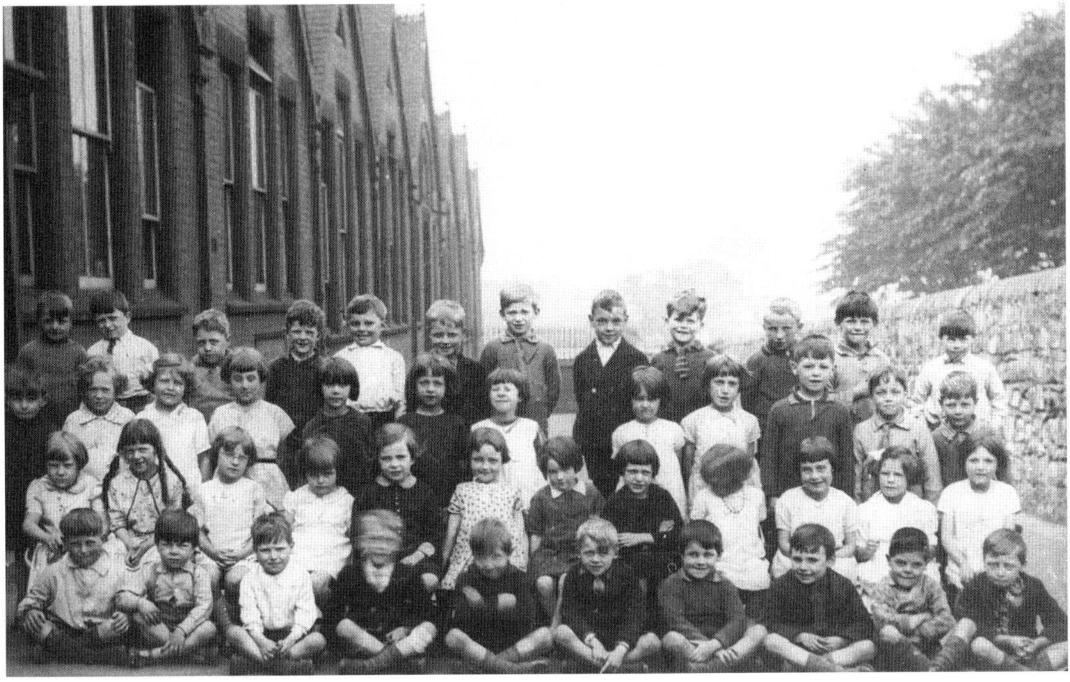

Above and below: Two views of what is thought to be members of the homeguard. In the top picture they are seen at Belle Vue, Doncaster Rovers ground, and below at Scarborough Barracks at the rear of South Parade seen in the background. Wormald (1973) states:

'The town was never under heavy attack from the air and in the five years [of the Second World War] only about twenty incidents were recorded in the Control ranging from parachute mines in May, 1941 (the most tragic with over twenty deaths) to a shower of incendiary bombs on Hyde Park in 1942...'

Above: Men in Waterdale with the Municipal High School for Girls in the background.

Below: Market traders. The picture was taken by local photographer, Luke Bagshaw (1875-1944), probably from an upstairs room in the Red Lion Hotel, looking towards Sunny bar. Luke was commissioned by the wholesale greengrocer and fruiterer, W.E. Cox.

Members of the Doncaster Mines Rescue Station.

Doncaster station staff. The year 1849 brought the main line from London and in his *Railways in South Yorkshire* (1975), C.T. Goode states:

'The original station at Doncaster consisted of two platforms each of 460ft in length served by loops off the through running lines...With the approach of the SY [South Yorkshire Railway] into the station a larger one was evolved having three main platforms, two, as now, serving northbound trains each side of an island. There were also four bays, two at the south end of the up and two at the north end of the down platform... The improved station was liberally provided with booking offices on both the up and down sides respectively.'

A scene at the Trades and Labour Club.

Doncaster Corporation Tramway Dept's staff. In 1898, the Doncaster Corporation obtained power under the Light Railway Act 1896 to operate electric tramways within the old Soke as defined in the Charters and, under the Order, a number of tram routes were opened from June 1902. The impetus was given in Doncaster by the development of electricity. A large generating station required a large consumption to be economic and this led the Corporation, among other factors, to obtain powers to construct electric tramways.

Doncaster Corporation Tramway Dept's maintenance staff. Gradually, the trams suffered increasing competition from motorbuses, and even converted vans and covered lorries operating unscheduled services along the tram routes. A serious fall in receipts, coupled with an increasing problem of track deterioration, led the Corporation to make several far-reaching decisions. They not only decided to abolish plans to extend the network to Hatfield, Rossington and Armthorpe, but to gradually eliminate tram services. The last tram to run in Doncaster was on the Brodsworth route on 8 June 1935.

Some of the women involved in war work during the First World War.

eight

Redevelopment

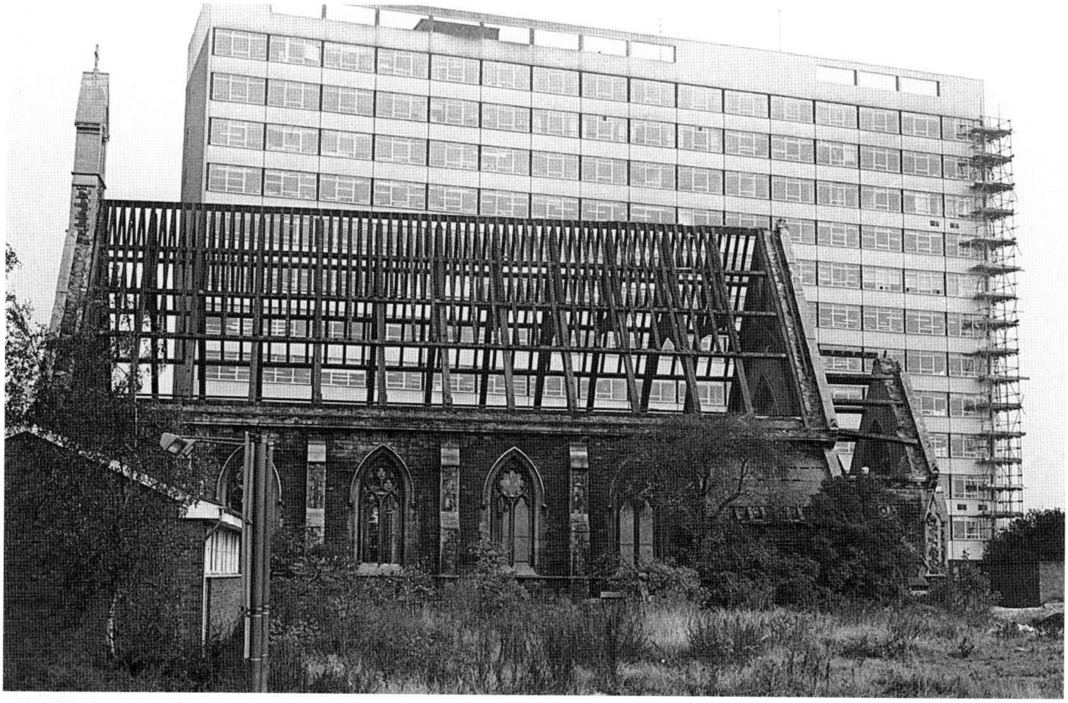

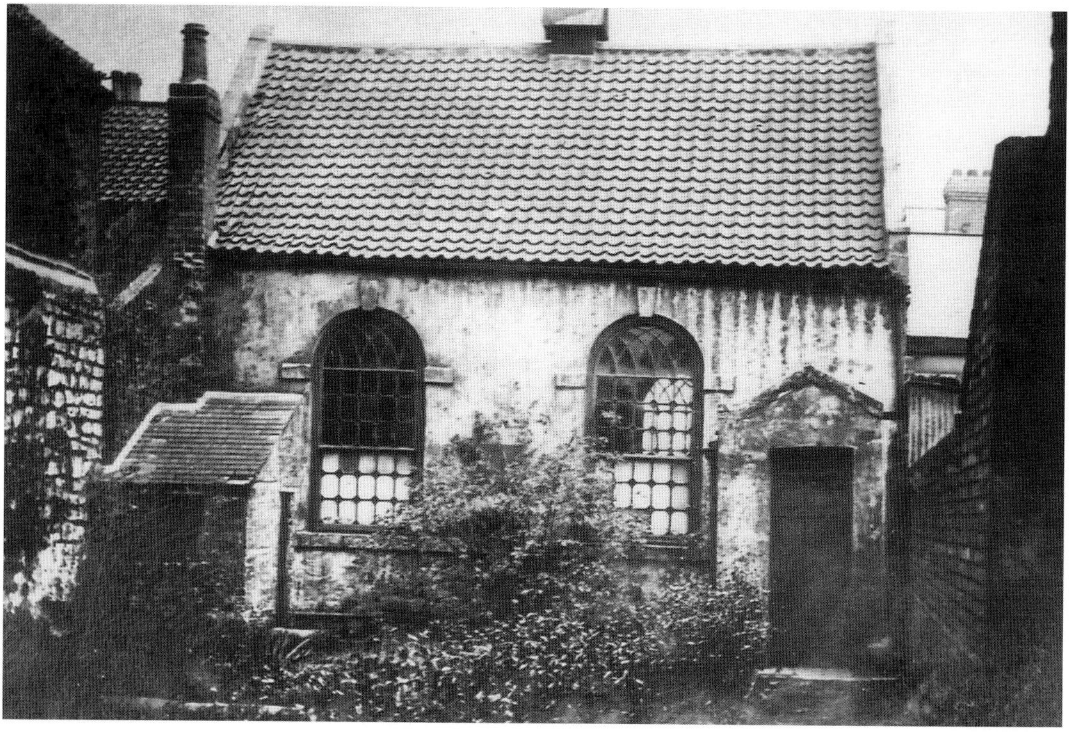

Above: Properties on Cleveland Street situated between Printing Office Street and Duke Street, in around 1982, shortly before the demolition to facilitate the Colonnades development.

Opposite above: The National Progressive Spiritualist Church is being demolished on Catherine Street (now College Road). Coal House (now Council House) is in the background.

Opposite below: The Unitarian Church, formerly situated between Hall Gate and Wood Street, was replaced by another structure, the Free Christian Church, in 1912.

Above: Work taking place on the removal of the Common Pond during the early 1920s. The view is looking towards Carr House Road, which was subsequently extended westwards from this point.

Opposite above: The demolition of the model shop owner Bernard Cuttriss's premises on Cleveland Street during the early 1960s. Bernard, along with his sons Michael and David, moved their operation a short distance away to Duke Street, where it survived until November 1983.

Opposite below: Construction taking place on the new DHSS premises in Wood Street during the mid-1990s. The rear of Harwood Terrace, Warterdale, may be seen in the distance.

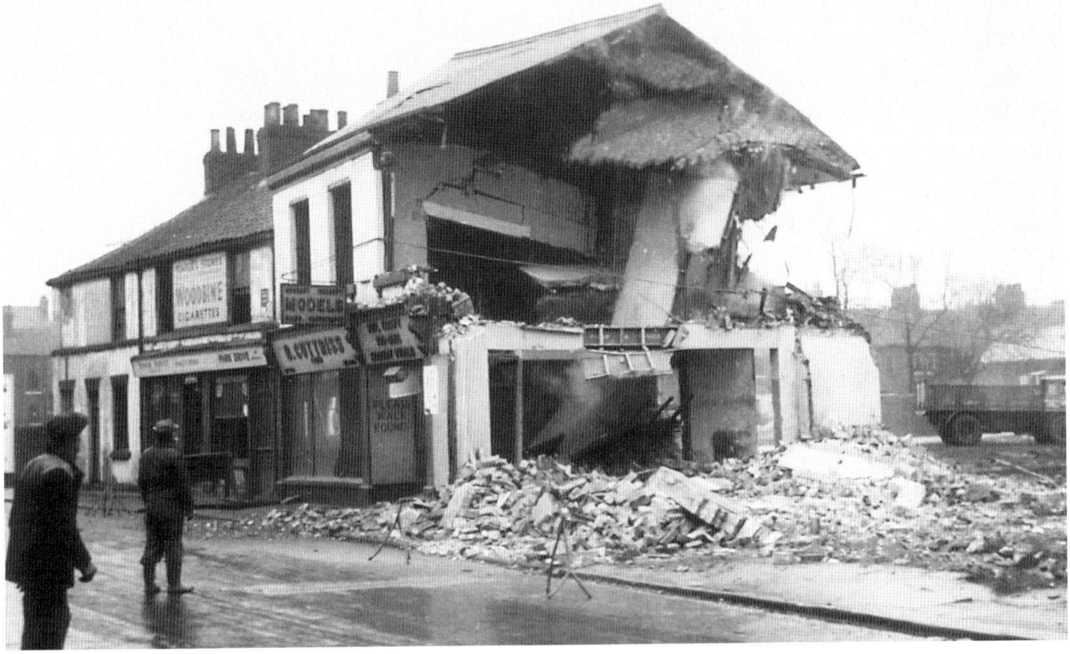
WOODBINE
CIGARETTES
MODELS

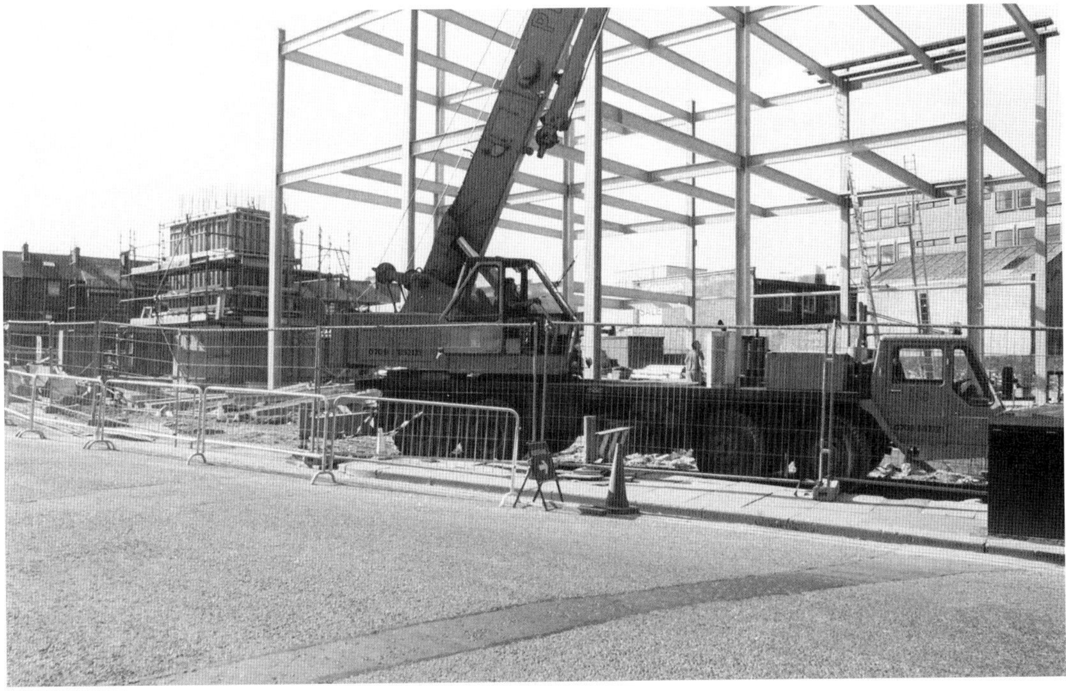

The Duke Street/Cleveland Street corner where unfit properties are being demolished, *c.* 1935

The Duke Street/Cleveland Street junction with the Cleveland Hotel in the distance on the left, in the early 1960s. Work in the foreground is concentrated on the construction of the ABC cinema forming part of the Golden Acres site. The two power station chimneys are visible on the horizon.

Looking east, with Friendly Street and the Crown & Anchor public house to the left and High Fisher Gate running horizontally in the foreground. Much of the area was redeveloped for the construction of the East by-pass and a car park. The pub had existed on the site from at least 1832.

Looking towards the Francis Street/East Laith Gate junction, with redevelopment taking place during the 1980s.

The old infirmary (latterly Education Offices) at the Whittaker Street/Wood Street junction being demolished during 1995. The event caused a rumpus in the town, with many feeling the building ought to have been put to some further use.

A new subway being made during the early 1960s for access to the new Arndale (later French Gate) Centre. The view is looking towards French Gate and the Olde Barrel Café may be identified.

Development taking place during the early 1960s on the Golden Acres site. The view is facing Waterdale (on the right) and part of the area in the foreground was to become the Southern bus station.

Subway construction extending between the St James Street flats and the Green Dyke Lane Cemetery around the 1970s. On more than one occasion, redevelopment in this area of the town was formidable because of the extensive underground works that formed part of the marvellous Sandhouse workings.

Another view of the Golden Acres development, this time looking towards the Cleveland Street/Duke Street junction.

A Littlewoods store under construction in Baxter Gate. The store opened on 2 May 1974.

The Bridge Hotel at the centre of the picture is undergoing demolition during the early 1970s. Properties in Marsh Gate to the right are also awaitng clearance.

Excavation work taking place during the construction of the Southern bus station. In the distance is the Spring Gardens Methodist chapel at the Spring Gardens/Cleveland Street junction.

Demolition work taking place at St James (The Plant) Schools near Hexthorpe Bridge, *c.* 1988. These schools were rebuilt after a fire in 1895, opening on 9 March 1897. The Great Northern Railway Co. contributed towards the costs. The new school was erected by Arnold & Sons and only accommodated girls. Boys were housed in a new school off Green Dyke Lane. A clock tower in the girl's school was erected in memory of the Plant Works Locomotive Manager, John Shotton.

St James Street facing the town centre with new flats on the left and old properties, which were later demolished, on the right. St James Street once extended from Waterdale to the Shakespeare's Head public house at the junction with St Sepulchre Gate. In 1961, shortly before demolition began, the Doncaster Directory for that year listed 148 properties on the thoroughfare.

Two views of the Doncaster Co-operative Society's building in Station Road being demolished *c.* 1970. Station Road was formally opened on 31 August 1882, by Mayor Charles Verity and members of the Corporation. The Co-op was built in 1887.

Work taking place during the 1960s on a subway stretching between the railway station, out of view to the right, and the new Arndale Centre. In the background is the Edwards Motor Co., formerly known as W.E. Clark & Co. Ltd, and claiming to be the first concern to enter the motor trade in the town. W.E. Clark set up a small shop in Bennetthorpe, in which he was a blacksmith, also making and selling penny-farthing and safety bicycles. He was himself a keen cyclist, but later recognised there was a great future for the motor car, and he became one of the pioneer drivers. Like all other pioneers, he had to face scorn and ridicule. Before 1902 he had moved from his small premises in Bennetthorpe to larger ones in Hall Gate, and eventually to Station Road. R.L.D. Edwards was a son-in-law of W.E. Clark, who died in 1932.

Demolition of buildings on the north side of Branson Street, a short stretch of road leading from Hall Gate to Waterdale. Note the van belonging to Moore & Hooper passing on the right.

nine

Aerials

Aerial view of Beckett Road looking towards Wentworth Road with St Mary's Road on the bottom right, *c.* 1926. Note the tram standing at the outer terminus near Morley Road, which was only a few hundred yards from the Avenue Road tram terminus in Thorne Road. The Beckett Road route, with its rows of terraced houses, was much better tramway territory than Avenue Road and receipts were much higher. Despite this, however, the undertaking made no worthwhile profits until 1913 and had to offer various fare concessions in order to attract passengers. Also note that the east side of Auckland Road was not built upon at this time.

Here we are looking in a north-easterly direction with the main line railway to the left and the St Sepulchre Gate/Cleveland Street junction in the foreground, c. 1938. Interestingly we can see work taking place on the extension to the railway station and the construction of the Doncaster Co-operative Society's new store, at the St Sepulchre Gate/Printing Office Street junction, off centre to the right. The store was opened on Monday 9 December 1940. Sir William Bradshaw, President of the Co-operative Wholesale Society, who opened the premises, spoke of the faith of the pioneers of the Co-operative movement – a faith which he said had been fully justified. The new structure was referred to as 'Doncaster's Finest Building', and was an example of the Art Deco style of architecture. Not only did the new store embody many new ideas in its interior, but the building itself was also constructed on a principle almost completely new to this country at the time. This was the cantilever principle, by means of which the outside walls of the first three floors (the white glazed portion) are hung upon girders which project from the central mass of the building. It was said that the principle was similar to that of hanging gifts upon the branches of a Christmas tree. The president of the Doncaster Society, Cllr F.A. Richardson, said that twenty-five years earlier the Society decided to have the new premises at this site but the plans were held up by the Corporation's road-widening plans. Property was purchased and it was agreed to set back the building to allow street widening. Richardson also paid tribute to and expressed the Society's thanks to the architects, Messrs T.H. Johnson, Shinton Jones consulting engineer and Messrs Pilkington Bros for the glass work.

Above: North Bridge facing south *c.* 1926. Trafford Street to the right was laid out as a new street in around 1910.

Another view from around 1938, this time facing north. Noticeable in the foreground is a large structure housing the Ritz cinema. Also note demolition work taking place on the left, between Hall Gate and Wood Street.

Hall Gate extends to the left and East Laith Gate in its un-rebuilt state extends from the right to Sunny Bar, *c.* 1926. Note the large structure housing the Palace Theatre on Silver Street, cutting across the centre of the picture.

Above the North Bridge looking east in around 1938. This view clearly illustrates the new route of the river, cutting out the Devil's Elbow section, which was completed some four years earlier.

This old photograh shows the view over South Parade looking north with the Gaumont cinema under construction near the centre, c. 1934

The Station Road/St Sepulchre Gate junction with work taking place on the King's Arcade in the foreground, during the early 1920s.

This damaged image shows the High Street, with the Danum Hotel in the bottom right and Clock Corner top left, during the mid-1920s. Work can be seen taking place on the construction of the NatWest Bank and the setting back of the northern side of Scot Lane.

Station Road facing Printing Office Street, *c.* 1930.

South Parade with the Majestic cinema in the top left corner and South Belmont or The Lodge to the bottom right

St James Street with the Oxford Place Methodist Chapel to the right and Ream's Corporation Brewery to the far left.

Aerial view of Beechfield House and grounds and the Municipal High School for Girls in the foreground, c. 1936.

The Cleveland Street/High Street junction may be seen in the bottom right of this view, from around 1938.

St George's Church dominates this view, *c.* 1926. The Art School/Technical School may be seen on the left.

The view of Glasgow Paddocks, with various thoroughfares including Catherine Street, Bentinck Street and Cemetery Road cutting across, *c.* 1951. The Oxford Place Methodist Chapel may be seen in the bottom left hand corner.

St James Street looking towards the town centre with Camden street extending to the left, *c.* 1955. The John Street Co-op and Ream's Corporation Brewery are also on the left.

The view facing the town centre with the Co-op building off centre to the right and redevelopment taking place in the foreground in Union Street (now truncated) and Cleveland Street, in the early 1960s.

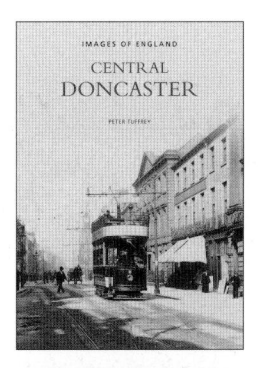

Other local titles published by Tempus

Central Doncaster
PETER TUFFREY

In the twentieth century a number of the Doncaster's long established thoroughfares were widened, shopkeepers updated their premises, a tramway system was opened and the North Bridge replaced the railway level crossing. Later, large-scale rebuilding replaced much nineteenth-century housing and central Doncaster was designated a modern commercial and business area. Peter Tuffrey's first book of old photographs on Doncaster is a nostalgic record of this city through these important years.
0 7524 3016 5

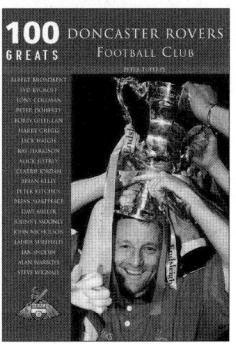

Doncaster Rovers FC 100 Greats
PETER TUFFREY

There will always be some debate as to what constitutes a great player, and what criteria might be used for their selection. This book features greats from each decade, starting from the 1920s. Players in this selection include Tom Keetley, Peter Doherty, Darren Moore and Mark Atkins. The club's great days were undoubtedly when Doherty was at the helm and, for a time, under Billy Bremner. Players from that time and many more Doncaster Greats feature in this book.
0 7524 2707 5

South Yorkshire Coalfield: A History and Development
ALAN HILL

The first recorded evidence of coal mining in South Yorkshire dates from thirteenth century Mexborough and Silkstone and mining has been an important industry since then. The area covered by the South Yorkshire Coalfield was huge, running from Barnsley to Sheffield and Doncaster and beyond. As improvements in technology appeared, so the depths of seams worked became greater. Whilst little remains today as evidence of this industry, some opencast sites and old mining villages serve as a reminder of South Yorkshire's proud industrial history.
0 7524 1747 9

Bakewell and the White Peak
PETER TUFFREY

The 200 postcard views in this book were taken from the Edgar Leonard Scrivens collection. His pictures show local views prior to industrial or commercial developments, such as children playing in traffic-free streets, manor houses such as Chatsworth House, and well-known local landmarks including Man Tor at Castleton, and Lovers Leap at Stoney Middleton. Here, Bakewell and many of the surrounding areas, including Baslow, Beeley, Calver, Castleton, Grindleford and Rowsley are shown in their pre-industrial innocence.
0 7524 3042 4

If you are interested in purchasing other books published by Tempus, or in case you have difficulty finding any Tempus books in your local bookshop, you can also place orders directly through our website

www.tempus-publishing.com

or from   BOOKPOST, Freepost, PO Box 29, Douglas, Isle of Man, IM99 1BQ
tel 01624 836000   email bookshop@enterprise.net